I0190120

CHRISTIANITY

THE BASICS

ELGIN L. HUSHBECK, JR.

Topical Line Drives
Volume 27

Energion Publications
Gonzalez, Florida
2017

It is scientifically proven that life is prolonged
Eat fewer calories (sugar and refined flour) and increased
Nutrients:

High consumption of sugar, along with environmental pollution
And physical inactivity is the main culprits
Most chronic diseases that plague our
Society: diabetes, hypertension, atherosclerosis, obesity,
Cancer, Alzheimer's, and autoimmune diseases.
• The consumption of sugar is addictive. This is because
Tryptophan absorption decreases, which is the precursor
Serotonin. If we lack serotonin we become
Compulsive and anxious to eat carbohydrates, especially
Refined and this leads to obesity.
• Furthermore, sugar generates a state of acidosis and
Lack of oxygen in the cell.
In conclusion, one could say that the well-being or satisfaction
Providing sugar consumption in all its forms (flour,
Candy, soda, etc...) Is as ephemeral as harmful, so a
Good advice would be to decrease the intake of these products
and
Increase of semi-drying nuts, such as figs, dates,
Raisins, among others, which are less harmful to health.
Return to start
While sugar is directly recommended in the daily diet,
For those who cannot get used to, it is best not to absorb
Fast.
As for drinks, it will always be replaced by
Lemon water, and if you want by itself or stevia, and / or ginger,
and all
Types of fruit juices and fresh and raw vegetables.

At the same time, rather than candy, get in the habit
Eating dried fruits, with great nutritional value and calories.
Are the ideals? Walnuts, in combination with dried figs, are
Excellent for athletes and adolescents.
Always prefer whole grains, is a healthy choice. When

Survival, along with fear, anger, sadness, or happiness,
They have a specific purpose: preserving the physical integrity to
Threats to the human being, putting in place effective responses
And adaptive. FIGHT /FLIGHT. The problem is when these
Mechanisms are activated constantly for any real reason or
Apparent coming to destroy the emotions.
Emotions are a gift from God to man. But many
Times the misuse of them turns them into a deadly weapon against
Ourselves and others.
Statistically (magnitude of the problem)
* 20% of the world's population suffers from a disorder of
Anxiety.
 80% of depressed individuals suffer symptoms of
Anxiety. Apprehension unrealistic fears, eagerness, agitation,
Irritability and panic attack.
* 60% of people with depression suffer physical symptoms
Anxiety related headache, irritable bowel syndrome
Chronic fatigue, chronic pain.
* 65% of these people suffer from sleep problems.
Arriving to feel agitation, phobias, generalized anxiety,
Panic attacks.
Fear and anxiety can alter both our
Physical and emotional functioning. Also puts us in a
Spiritual bondage because they interfere in our relationship with
God.

Manifestations of anxiety:
Nervousness, retaining excessive, unwarranted sense of fear,
Insomnia, irritability, restlessness, inability to
Concentrate, panic. There are many recipes to relieve anxiety
And its effects ranging from exercise, manage stress
Adequately, and proper nutrition.

Sugar Effects not so sweet

Consequences of too much sugar

BAKED FISH: SEASONED OVERNIGHT
FOR BAKING ADDOLIVE OIL, GARLIC, CARROTS.
• VEGETABLESATE LENTIL. VEGETABLES ARE
BROCCOLI, CAULIFLOWER, TAYOTA, CARROT, GREEN
BEANS.
• SOY SALAD LASAGNA.
• FISH STEAMED WITH GARLIC + VEGETABLES.
• PASTA WITH SAUCE OF PESTO SALAD INTEGRAL.

• RICE, BEAN SOY MEAT.
• MIX RICE BEANSEGGPLANTSTEW.
• INTEGRAL RICE SATE LENTILS FISH.
• SOUP OF FISH AND VEGETABLES.
• TUNA SALAD SANDWICH.
• TUNA WITH PASTA SALAD
GREEN SALAD.
• POTATOES BAKED STUFFED WITH CHEESE
VEGETABLES.
• PEPPERS FILLINGS (FISH OR SOY).
SALAD.
• EGGPLANT WITH EGG VEGETABLE PIE

HEALTHY DINNER
1) VEGETABLE SOUP. (2 times a week).
2) GINGER TEA, CINNAMON, and ANISE. (3 times a week).
(3) LEMON CUCUMBER SHAKE. (2 times a week).
(4) ¼cup of dried seeds without salt. (4 times a week).

Stress and anxiety
From a Latin definition anxieties, anguish and grief:

Emotional response is mainly characterized by
a high degree of activation of the peripheral appearing
a number of observables and engines usually involve
behavior and poorly adjusted adaptive behavior.
Anxiety has a very important function connected with the

Caused such rancor and start to forgive one by one. If you recognize that you must forgive, feel free to ask for forgiveness, you will feel a relief.

List of purchase
Romaine lettuce, tomatoes, pepper, cucumbers, olives, peppers, Onion, natural garlic, cilantro, lemon, ginger, cinnamon, anise Honey, Aloe Vera. Balsamic vinaigrette dressing.
Tayota, green beans, eggplant, lentils, beans, soy,
Fish (tilapia). Organic eggs, organic soy milk, cheese
White, plain yogurt. PISTACHIOS, WALNUTS AND ALMONDS.
EXTRA Virgin olive oil.
Fruits: apples, grapes, strawberries, mango.
Brown rice, whole wheat bread, whole grain cereal, peanut butter
, green and ripe plantains, potatoes, small oats.

HEALTHY BREAKFASTS
• INTEGRAL CEREAL CHEESE TOAST GRAPE
APPLE.
• OATS WITH MILK TOAST, ADD
Strawberry WATHERMELON peanut butter.
• BANANA YOGURT FRIED EGG GRAPE STRAWBERRY.
• POTATOES BOILED CHEESE TOAST WITH
Strawberry MANGO peanut butter.

• OATMEAL BOILED EGG TOAST WITH
GRAPE Strawberry peanut butter.
• CEREAL CHEESE BANANA MANGO GRAPE.
• TOAST CEREAL CHEESE YOGURT STRAWBERRY
GRAPES.
• YOGURT POTATO BOILED EGG TOAST
GRAPE 1/2 BANANA.
HEALTHY LUNCH
• BAKED FISH SALAD.
THE SALAD HAS LETTUCE, TOMATO, CUCUMBER,
OLIVES AND FRESH THE BALSAMIC
VINAGRETTE.

8-) Do you have high blood pressure, diabetes or high cholesterol?

9-) Consumes cans (canned) products.

10. You eat foods from one or several days of preparations.

11 Consume sweets, candies, chocolates, chewing gum, Soda.

12 - Have 2 years or more without taking vacations.

13 Consume more than 2 cups of coffee a day.

14 Eat sugar or diet sugar.

Total unfavorable points.

INTERPRET THE TEST

Subtract the unfavorable to the favorable points.

If your score is - 2 to 14, your lifestyle need to changes Immediately. It is possible that you not to enjoy good health.

If you obtained a score of 3 to 14. You do some things well, I invite you to improve your lifestyle, you can do so much better and

Enjoy the benefits of a healthy lifestyle.

If your score is 15-24 your lifestyle is regular.

I invite you to do it all well to take an excellent lifestyle With more than 25 points in this test.

GET PEACE THROUGH FORGIVENESS.

Our emotions have an effect on our organism. It is necessary to forgive ourselves and forgive other

People. The most beneficial by the means of forgiveness is the person

Person that chooses to forgive is you. Time turns the Resentment and anger in poisons that are destroying the emotions of

People preventing them from being happy and making other people

Pay without any guilt.

Decide to forgive today. Make a list of people that you

Smile, surrounded by people with good disposition which motivate you
And serve as inspiration. Look for the comic side of life and behind
That side you'll be able to see things from a different crystal.

PERIODICALLY EVALUATE YOUR HABITS
TESTTOASSESSYOURLIFESTYLE.

Each question has a value, must answer it honestly.
If your answer is yes, then add 2 points to favorable habits.
If your answer is no add zero.

FAVORABLE habits (value 2 points each question).

1-) you eat 2 fruits every day.
2-) Sleep 7 hours a day.
3-) only eat whole-grain bread, integral brown rice.
.
4-) exclusively only use olive oil for cooking.
5-) Rests and relaxes once every week.
6-) Are a cheerful and optimistic person.
7-) usually have control of your emotions.
8-) You maintain a proper weight.
9-) Exercise 4-5 times during the week.
10-) Eat vegetables and salads every day.
11-) Practice any sport on a regular basis.
12-) Evacuate normal-looking stools every day.
 13-) Comes always to a usual time and form Regular.
14No grudge for anyone
TOTAL POINTS.

HABITOS DESFABORABLES (value 1 point each question). If
Yes, add 1 point, if your answer is no, add zero.

1 You are or live with a smoker.
2. You drink alcoholic beverages.
3 work more than 8 hours a day.
4 Have overweight.
5 You have problems sleeping.
6 Late nights with some frequency.
7 Eat meat more than 4 times in the week.

Negative, pessimistic, sad ways. Avoid being influenced in negative
Way.
CHANGE THE ENVIRONMENT IN THEIR FAVOR.
You can choose make changes in their environment in favor of your
health. Practical examples:
Open the window of where you work, if you don't have one take out
To take breath outside. If you smoke, quit smoking, if you drink alcohol
Refrain from doing so, if you have a bad alimentation improve
You're feeding. Learn about a better way of life, one more
Healthy.
We change our environment to our favor deciding
To improve our way of life with determination. By removing
Everyday habits that subtract the value of our lifestyle
(See test of your lifestyle later).
GET AN ANNUAL PHYSICAL EXAMINATION.
It is of utmost importance to attend regularly without fear of the doctor.
It is this control that can help the physician find in
An early stages any health problem. A style of
Healthy lifestyle does not guarantee that we won't get sick of something
At some point. What if I can assure you that the medicine
Works better in a healthy body. It is necessary to mention that
Our attitude makes the difference in the adverse situations that
Life presents.
CONTINUE TO IMPROVE YOUR HEALTH.
Attend workshops of nutrition or health, take courses in health,
Buy a book that will help you to continue to improve feeding
And lifestyle. Investigate how to prevent diseases.
ALWAYS KEEP A GOOD ATTITUDE.
Have this recommendation always present. The people who
Have a positive attitude live longer and are in better health.

Consciously and make concrete plans from the perspective of life,

Improve your lifestyle.

Use resources such as:

Reflexology of the foot, music therapy, color therapy, aroma

Therapy, are of great help for combating stress.

TAKE SUN REGULARLY.

The Sun is a source of energy, through it we can acquire the

Vitamin D naturally, this star is essential for our

Survival. The best time to sunbathing is from the dawn

until11:00 a.m. and then from 3:00 pm until sun set. Take Sun for

15 minutes a day at least. This brings

Multiple benefits to your health, lets cite a few of these:

1-) Strengthens bones and teeth.

2-) Improves the appearance of skin.

3-) Stimulates the immune system.

4-) People who take Sun suffer less from depression,

Because it increases the secretion of serotonin.

5-) Improves the quality of sleep.

6-) Balances the levels of cholesterol in blood.

7-) Increases testosterone levels in the blood.

AVOID TOXINS

Avoid smoking, alcohol (2 ounces of wine 4 times

Per week maximum). Toxic are also dyes

And artificial sweeteners, canned, chemical of some dyes for hair beauty products, creams,

Soaps, toothpaste, deodorants with anti tranpirat deodorants (used without

Antiperspirant) these are associated with many diseases.

By what we recommend to use which are manufactured based on

Natural products.

Try listening to music at adequate levels of sound. Levels

Very high cause increase of stress and are considered as

Contamination of the environment. Some songs contaminate the

Person because they have a content that leads them to think of

Family, or simply practice some sport, do not leave
Taking your day off every week.
(3) Monthly rest, visit a spa, retreat to the countryside, visit a
Museum, participate in any social or charitable work, participate in
A marathon or rally.
(4) Rest annual, are holidays. It is necessary to plan
These holidays. When your vacations is finished you feel with
New strength.

If you are suffering from a sleep disorder problem
You should seek professional help as soon as possible.
MANAGE YOUR STRESS PROPERLY.
It is a physiological reaction of the organism in which come into play
Various defense mechanisms to deal with a situation which is
perceived as threatening or of increased demand.
Stress is natural and a necessary response for survival.
This natural response is given in excess, occurs when once
Retention overloads and appears diseases and abnormalities in
Abnormal operation. Anxiety is a stress response
Sustained and poorly managed.
Some foods we eat may increase the levels of
Stress and anxiety. Many people show high levels of
Stress by eating large amounts of food or eating
Constantly as a form of stress relief. The combination of
Carbohydrate and sugar is preferred and promotes an environment
Favorable for anxiety and stress to be addictive and easy
Access.
We recommend in this regard the following:
Plan fun activities, take regular breaks, and find positive
situations, moderate exercise, and a good
Alimentation (balanced), do not eat too much, socialize with
Other persons, use of relaxation techniques, practicing yoga
Exercise, meditate, and take time for leisure activities, live

At this time the breathing is more superficial, heartbeat is slow and weak. This is what is called circadian or biological rhythms, are variations of the physiological rhythm
(Metabolic rate, heat production, flowering) of all the
Living beings. This proves once again that our body works in conjunction with our planet and their movements
Rotation and translation in time and space coordinate with
The entire universe. For this reason it is important and healthy that
We are well tuned with our environment.
We recommend also:
To not watch television before bedtime, or have a TV within the Bedroom. The majority of television programs are
Designed to capture their attention to preventing in this sense
That some people sleep properly. Avoid listening
Or watching news within hours of going to bed, since sleep is
Under negative influences it is unhealthy and could activate the
Alert systems and generate more stress that already generated
During the day. TV commercials are designed
To work through this subconscious and awakening method
Making an apparent need to consume these products.

Prepare a pleasant environment to go to sleep. A
Pleasant temperature, with little or no lighting will help
You understand it is the hour of a desired rest.
Put your electronics such as a cell phone, radio and computer equipment to
More than 3 meters from where you are resting.
If you feel comfortable to put instrumental music for sleep or
Rest. You can also place any scent that is to your liking.
From a shower with warm water before going to bed. Put your
Mind positive and think of some time, place or circumstance
You remember or imagine that are pleasant.
Avoid lying down with the stomach full; this bad habit subtraction has much to
With your health.
(2) It is the weekly rest, on your day off go to the Park, visit some

REST.

The rest is one of the most effective medicines. When a
Patient is admitted to a the hospital is one of the therapies
That applies immediately as arriving. To the rest of our body
Replenishes energy not eating more than we replace energy
as many do. During this process of our organism we
can be relieved and ready to start again. If we
notice, the rest is the cornerstone to having a healthy lifestyle.
Most people suffering from any disorder
Sleep or cannot rest suffer progressive deterioration
and accelerated in comparison with those who did manage to
sleep and
rest.
****
****
Some of the effects of deprivation of rest are irritability,
Cognitive impairment, loss of memory, hallucinations,
Deterioration of the immune system, increases the risk of
diabetes
Type 2, heart rate variability, increases the risk of heart attacks
, decreases the ability to react in time and
Precision, increased pain, suppression of growth, increases the
Risk of obesity, decreased body temperature, between
Others.
There are 4 types of rest which I want to talk to you in this
Opportunity.

1-) the daily rest period, is when we lay down to sleep all
Every day. It is advisable to sleep at least 7 hours a day.
Time to go to sleep should always be at the same time
And not move from 11:30 pm. This is to make a daily habit
And get sleepy at that time, in addition to when lying down
Already at that time at 3:00 am in the morning you will be
entering in a deep sleep and would rest properly.

That the majority of people are not consistent with exercise and this makes it still demanding having as many calories resulting in a sudden weight gain.

Accustom your body to a diet high in calories
day may turn out to be2-edgedweapon, everything is fine until
you leave the exercises for whatever reason. Many people try
exercising to lose weight but have not taken into account that one day your body will be tired of being subjected to both
exercise and result in not pursuing but rather than quitting. Joints
and cartilages, bones, tendons, muscles and nerves are part of the system that allows movement; they are not designed to beeter nale specially when used too much and so intense. Intense physical exercise is not the right way to lose weight. Wrong and misguided people
are making a many big mistakes.

Other people have time constraints and unable to attend to the Gym 5 times a week as it is required. In other cases the Physical or health limitations prevent them from exercising intensely
And for extended periods.

For these and other reasons we recommend exercise immodest form, never exceeding 45 minutes four to five times a week.
If it is possible to do so in a park or open space. If you are unable to
Then on a treadmill but do it.

The best time to walk is during the morning, but if you cannot Do it in the afternoon or at night.
\

Do not count any other drink as a glass of water such as
Coffee or tea.

In that sense it is allowed to consume up to 2 cups of coffee or tea
Per day (rate of 4 oz).

BREATHEFRESH AIR.

Air is vital in a healthy lifestyle. Human beings
We are not designed to live enclosed and poorly ventilated.
We recommend opening the windows of the house, specifically where
We are bedroom, place of work or go out to intake air.
Maintain a proper body position allowing a good
Breathing, and make respiratory exercises. These consist in of the
Follows:

Inhale deeply; hold the air in your lungs
Up to 3 and then release it gently through your mouth, repeat 12-15
Times every day, mainly to get up and go to bed.

Visit places where you can breathe clean air as the Park, the
Field where there are trees.

Exercise regularly MODERATE
In this healthy lifestyle we recommend a moderate exercise.
It is the exercise that stifles us it does not entails our effort
Greater than our capacity and state of fitness. Example: walk during
30 to 45 minutes at moderate pace. One of the problems that

We have observed is that too many people are exercised and
This increases your daily caloric requirements. The problem is

You should drink 6 to 8 glasses of 8 oz. a day. When you are thirsty
Frequently and without satiety of water this can result from a diet high in salt, some
Metabolic or endocrine imbalance. We do not recommend exceeding
This amount of water per day.

We recommend a following scheme for drinking water:

(1) One to two cups in the morning, help clean your stomach
The saliva and stomach juices accumulated during the night,
Thus preparing it for breakfast.

Activate your metabolism and help it to defecate with higher
Frequency and ease.

2-) two glasses at 11 am. Will help you to clean your stomach before
Lunch. It will also keep you hydrated,
This will prevent having to take water or liquids during the
Meals.

3-) two glasses at 3:00 pm (or after 2 hours of having
Lunch) emptied the rest of food remaining in the
Stomach after lunch leaving this without waste.

4-) two glasses at 6:00 pm, help maintain good
Hydration during the remaining hours.

The intention of this scheme is that we are not passing through
tall drinks of water, you can stay hydrated, do not need to take fluids while feeding, and avoid drinking during the night after going to bed and do not have to get up to urinate and disrupt your rest.

Eat Smart: the portion sizes and quantities
Recommended for different foods.
Distorted portions

DO FASTING PERIODICALLY.

One of the best medicines is to fasting. We recommend that you do
not fast with the intention to reduce weight but rather to give you a
rest to your digestive system. We recommend that fasting is every 15 days with the following specifications:

Start the day before fasting. Do not eat anything from
6:00 pm to 12: 00 am the next day. You can drink water. Do not
Drink coffee that day.

Also since you're not eating meditate or reflect.

Break the fast with some liquid and hot soup or something
Light.

DAYS OF DETOXIFICATION.

6 Natural juices of fruits that are to your taste buds, you can
Mix or match. Each juice should be no more or less of
16 ounces. Take one every two hours starting the first with
breakfast. This must be done every 15 days.

WATER CONSUMPTION.

The water we consume should be of good quality. Read the
Ingredients on the label and look to have no sodium. If you have
a
Filter at home replace the filter according to the specifications of
the
Manufacturer.

These recommendations are focused so that you consume the right amount of calories during the day and the night. While coming to a night's rest already your system will not contain as much calories. In avoiding with this that your body stores the remaining energy in the form of fat during the night.

Distorted portions

Currently, people eat more of what they used to and much more than they need. This means that they are constantly assimilating more calories than that their bodies can burn. Unfortunately, many of us do not warn ourselves that we are eating too much because we have much accustomed to see (and eat!) large portions. The portion sizes have increased over the past 20 years. The price of this overabundance is high. It is known that the people who commit systematic excesses to eating are likely

To be overweight. But they also risk suffering various Problems of health, including high blood pressure, high cholesterol, Type 2 diabetes, bone and joint problems, disorders Respiratory and sleep, and even depression. In the future, the People who commit excesses while eating are at increased risk to Get heart disease, heart failure and vascular Brain.

It is easy to understand why the restaurant industry tends to Serve more food than necessary: customers love to Feel that they are getting the best for your money! But The value of the meals is not a good deal if it triples Our calorie and paves the way for health problems. So, what you can do to regain control? A good Point to start is to know two things that may help you to

During lunch and dinner do not eat fruit, only during the breakfast.

Remove sugar from your diet, since it provides empty calories (without
antioxidant) Note read the chapter the on harmful effects of sugar.
Replace this with the natural sweeteners when necessary (agave syrup) or honey as long as is not in a hot drink. Do not use artificial sugar. Do not eat sweets,
gum, sodas; juices made industrially (prepare your
own juices with natural fruits). A good investment is a
juice processor.

Do not eat meat (beef, pork, chicken, fish, Turkey...) more than 2 times a week. Since the proteins of animal origin have a long period of digestion. Also this can be replaced without problems by protein of non-animal origin.

Avoid reheating food in microwave in plastic utensils.
Instead use special microwave-safe ceramic or glass.

Periodically change the cooking pots and utensils from your kitchen (every 2-3 years) according to their use. Do not use aluminum pots and pans
or that contain lead? Avoid using plastic spoons to move hot foods, instead use wood and replace
frequently.

Time limit for dinner is 8:00 pm; this is so that when you
lie down your stomach is already empty.

Place food in non-visible places, inside cabinets
or pantries. Never leave cooked food or easy to prepare in the refrigerator.

example: If you are going to drive 300 miles you need to replace gasoline for the vehicle, the breakfast is also that fuel that the body needs to start the day.

Lunch: combine salads and proteins or vegetables and proteins.

Dinner: we recommend that it is as light as possible. Seeds, tea, a soup.
Note: Read healthy menus.

As a rule of thumb do not drink water or any liquid 45 minutes before, during or after eating.

Do not consume energy drink; it is not needed in a style healthy lifestyle. Eating is a process that requires the following:

Do not perform other activity when eating.

Avoid eating if you're not hungry.

If you've had a shock or strong emotion, postpone the alimentation until you're calmed down completely.

Chew food thoroughly so that they are well digested and assimilated.

Use your hand to measure the portions of food that you have to eat at each meal. If something fits in your hand is not because it is
too much for you.

cells, this process takes place at this very moment in all your body and for this process to be healthy (from a
Cell, create a cell identical) it is necessary that these substances pro
Biotic are present in our food.

Devitalized products and that you should avoid eating:

Very processed foods, white flours, canned meal
prepared of several days, supplements, synthetic proteins, dietary formulas.

Instead we recommend:

Consume food as soon as possible after being prepared.
Do not store food made more than 24 hours of having been prepared.
Eat natural products.
Use olive oil, keep in mind should not be heated to high temperature (not more than 450 degrees)
Eat whole grains exclusively.
Another aspect that should be taken into consideration is to only eat
3 servings of meals a day breakfast, lunch and dinner.

Avoid Eating between meals, this will greatly benefit because it will avoid
that your digestive system is overloaded and restarting the process
constantly. Always eat at a specific time of day and
Wait this time to feed.

Breakfast: it is the most important meal of the day. You must include
2 natural fruits, cereal, protein (obtained from milk and its) derivatives). This food should be the strongest of the day. An

There are rules for good nutrition

The Quality of what we eat matters.
The amount of what we eat is vital.
What time we eat.
With that frequency.
How foods are made.
The proportion.
How we combine foods.

Care quality, quantity of what they eat and the time at which it is consumed. In this regard, you should always prefer quality products,
eat only the amount that is necessary for you and only eat at the established hours. Avoid eating spontaneously and without need.

Read the nutritional information of the products it consumes as well
as the ingredients it contains will help you to choose the best.

Avoid drinking very processed foods because these do not
Contain the amount of nutrients that your body needs.
Food devitalized and devoid of pro-biotic substances fill the stomach, but they do not have the ability to generate life.
Some contain many chemicals and additives. A
Practical example: If you sow a bean of a Tin can in the dirt
This can be born and give rise to a plant? Of course not. By the
Contrary, if you sow naturally a plant can be born. This
Simple example helps us understand the following: the first
Bean is not capable of giving life, and already died long ago,
It remains rotting by the preservatives that were added.

The second is capable of generating life and has all the properties
Our body needs since our cells are being
reproducing constantly and giving birth to other generations Of

We could help our body, to eliminate with greater
ease the toxic waste having a better diet.

Food is a habit, so you can
Re-educate it and can make changes to make it
balanced with the proper knowledge and application.

Today there are thousands of products on the shelves of
supermarkets, thousands of options for food.
However, not all have good quality.
Some of them were created for the purpose of "satisfying
a need, to remove the hunger" and were not
healthy, for what, fundamental today more
than ever choosing food correctly.

The food is a habit that is inherited. Families have the
same habit of feeding. It is no coincidence to get
sick of the same. Added to what was said above there are
different cultural, religious habits, traditions
styles according to the geographical location.
The different ways of feeding ourselves are a studies motive,
buying the habits of feeding different people (villages) and
cultures it is known that there are populations who enjoy a better
health. Feeding themselves, the factor that mostly influences
health
of the person it is time to pay attention to the value that we give
to ours and to learn of every culture the positive habits that
lets us be able to apply.

We recommend not go to the supermarket hungry because
under these
circumstances, the trend is to buy products to consume
quickly. To avoid this carry a list of purchases. You know
what you are eating in advance. Food should not be
on the fly. Also take into account the following
aspects:

CHAPTER 4
GOOD FOOD

It is necessary to know that the food is a habit
Most important influence on our health, it is for this reason
That we must pay special attention.

Alimentation:
"The power begins with the selection of
Food at the grocery store or market".

The value we give to our food is decisive.
The people who cherish their power do not eat
everything they want, nor at any time, to have food with value
high enough that leads them to be aware.

What is the purpose of food? It is to resupply
in a balanced manner the energy demands for
that our body for functioning properly.

When we are not aware of the impact of the
food in our health, we simply eat
deliberately overloading our body with energy
that is not necessary and will have to turn into "something", in a
final product that will be stored or deposited in any
place. In this sense we can refer to a concept
physical "energy is not only destroyed transforms", this
can be applied to food because food is
converted into energy that is then used by our body. With
certainly, the excesses in our diet will have an
impact on our health. Thus, when consumed
food is that they do not have a good quality or are very
processed. The disposal of these products is required
part of our body waste. Our body has the ability to get rid of
many of these toxic residues in the majority of cases, but not all.
This
also depends on the State of health by the person.

person succeed in life regardless of discipline.

3-) Set a goal, will serve you as a stimulus to continue
day by day.

4-) do not pass unnoticed details many times these are those
that make the real difference.

5-) Prepare for the comments of other people that will give you
words of encouragement, but others may try to discourage you.

6-) Overcome it, there will be moments that you will have
to fight with yourself.

7-) Encourages others to begin as well, help make skills.

8-) Tell others that you have decided to start a new style
of life. Commit it to others.

9-) if you fall get up and continue, don't ever lose hope,
this is the goal for those who are awake.

10-) periodically evaluate your achievements, this will stimulate
you to continue.

communicates to us with the
exterior leaves and enters our body may be in favor or in
against with the balance that we need as living beings.

Most people know only some of the factors
that related to their disease. We educate ourselves and try to
learn from other people who made mistakes during
long and the sick did not establish a direct relationship
of his suffering with what they usually did what caused
no good, thus losing valuable information that would serve to
prevent a disease. Example of this is that there are cultures that
they have a high incidence of cancer, while in others
the incidence of this disease is much lower. So we could
make comparisons and relationships between the factors most
preponderant and decisive to make the difference.

We have designed a lifestyle taking into consideration the
factors most important in cultures that apparently promote good
health and to apply them correctly
oriented to provide a healthy lifestyle. In a way
we have identified some of the factors that do not promote
our health and well-being for which as far as possible and with
conscious recommend to replace them. In this way we can raise
the amount of factors Pro-health and reduce to lowest terms
that affect health.

Now it is the time to begin changing our life style,
habits and customs to live healthy and full of energy and vitality.
This depends on you.

Chapter 3 before Beginning

Bear in mind the following 10 points.
1-) should bear in mind the Word change. If you're not ready to
make changes you will remain having the same results obtained
so far.
2-) have discipline. Will be of much use, I have not seen any

preserving a

good health since this will determine how they will be our future

generations. We have to not only pass on good genes but also a culture aware of the importance of health as a means of preserve our species. Mechanisms to adapt to the environment are not fast enough compared with a

world that seems to be going at the speed of light when the laws of physics

they do not allow us to go changing at such speed.

Some people think that they are already condemned to suffer a medical condition, because there were already people in their family

with an illness and are only a matter of time for

that person to begin to show symptoms. This continues to be true,

although not in its entirety, thanks to which our genes can be modified, we can make this modification it is oriented

to produce better health. We have two options: the first is lower the chances of developing the disease by means a healthy lifestyle, or it may be that the disease

are present, but with a degree of severity less than what it would be presented. The second is: surrender and expect that the worst will happen in

without doing anything to prevent it. Are not condemned, until we exhaust all the resources we have available, which offer a healthy lifestyle.

Our environment is everything that has direct
or indirect contact with our body. Our food, culture,
Philosophy of life, habits, as well as everything which

doctor will ask some questions regarding your medical record and the current history of how you began feeling sick. The doctor will start ordering tests with the aim of establishing a diagnosis to the disease. Once you're diagnosed the doctor will prescribe that medicine that will cure the disease. However, you will remain in the same environment, without making any necessary changes and with the same style of life. Within the time of treatment if the disease is chronicle, of assurance it will get worse and you'll need more aggressive treatments. Despite this, you will continue with this lifestyle until the rest your days.

If you could change your lifestyle, to another much healthier with assurance that the results will be very different, because what produced the disease is no longer affecting it more. The best
treatment for a disease is to remove what produces it. Abad quality of life is the final outcome of unhealthy lifestyle not healthy. Both genes and the environment and our attitude are determinants. An approach from various points is needed for understanding how to prevent and treat diseases.
Statistics say that diabetes, cancer, circulatory diseases, immunological, obesity, asthma, allergies among others, continue wreaking havoc in the lives of the people, it is a clear signal that our genes which we inherited from past generations they were affected significantly and our environment.
It is much less favorable for us today; therefore,
if there's a refocus in continue of transmitting genes ever most defective to our last generations which will be
less healthy than what we are today. There may be a solution this situation and the implementation of a new lifestyle,
one more healthy and conscious of the importance of

Chapter 2

Identify the problem

The current health problems are multifactorial. It is much necessary to know which factors affect our health, as those that promote the same. Avoid as possible those who affect us and to cultivate those who benefit us. The more we can determine which hurts us and cultivate those that benefits; in the same measure we can increase our opportunities to live healthy.

Culture, our personal intuition, religion which we belong, our geographical location, the place in which we live, our philosophy; they have an influence on our way of life. This way every individual plans its form of life, their particular lifestyle which is understood to be their best choice without assessing the results of it, by adopting their ancestors' habits and customs. It is not a coincidence that families get sick and die of the same causes.

Nevertheless we have an enormous potential and the fact is that we can change the results when we apply a healthy life style.
"The ambience can modify our genes".

When we learn to replace the factors that affect us by those who favor us, only a matter of time will let us begin to enjoy the benefits of a healthy body.

Many people who attend consultation with a doctor can note the following:

Suppose you have a health problem, the consultation usually begins evaluating you the patient the signs and symptoms for the doctor to establish a diagnosis of a disease. Generally, the

Chapter 1   Mind   Body

               Alimentation

Health

To find a definition to what is thought to be health I must admit that the majority
of definitions are missing something to fully define a concept as important. However, the formal definition that gives the World Health Organization has varied over time in order to encompass a more complete definition. Health is a state of physical, mental and social well-being, with operating capacity, and not only the absence of disease or infirmity". It can also be defined as the level of functional or metabolic efficiency of the body both at the micro level (cellular) as to macro level (social). In 1992 an Investigator expanded the definition of WHOM, by adding: "and in harmony with the environment".

In General, health can be analyzed in 2 perspectives: physical health and mental health. These
maintain a close relationship at all times.

You have heard say: we are what we eat. This It is absolutely true, but I understand that we are more than that. We are what we feel, think, how we interpret, interact as living beings, what we do, perceive by our senses: vision, hearing, touch, sense of smell, as well as where we come from and where we live. By this reason we have life. Everything that surrounds us impacts and

It is involved in every one of the vital processes thus causing an effect pro-life (a favorable environment) or on the contrary work against pro-lifers (creating an unfavorable environment) causing our bodies struggle to adapt to the environment. We can make oriented changes to and in this way promote better health. The solution is not getting another planet, but rather care better what we already have, it starts with the education of each oriented individual in the same direction Pro-life. This way we will be able to learn to be better managers of what nature offers us, life.

This book is a compilation that attempts to unite the knowledge of conventional medicine and alternative medicine without underestimating. None of the knowledge that applied have real results with what we have created a new style of life to get people to learn to transform the

environment for your health and will live healthier.

Preface

HOW TO LIVE HEALTHY

During decades the human being has thought about how to
have a better quality
of life and of health. In the history of the humanity the illnesses
have claimed thousands of lives. Some of these illnesses as the
infectious and contagious could be controlled. Nevertheless,
other illnesses are present and have remained in increase.
Diabetes, cancer, cardiac, autoimmune diseases, circulation,
high blood pressure, arthritis, diseases of psychological origin,
Alzheimer's among others. Despite of the scientific advances
and the efforts to control these illnesses Continue to increase
each day. New medicines and treatments appear to address the
health problems, but what really is the cause of illness? Will we
be able to do anything more ourselves? I understand it is time
to change our way of facing and fighting with these conditions
to confront them with a good prevention by looking further
away at the apparent causes and to accept its real causes.

"Every person is born with a number of default health by genes,
these can be influenced and modified by the environment".

Most of these diseases are preventable, if we do a correct
prevention. The human body is capable of giving a response to
any stimuli in the environment; in it was conceived, born,
grows, develops until it dies. This response can be in defense, if
it considers that it is attacked, or by
the contrary can interact with what is in the environment if not
attacked creating a favorable environment for its balance,
survival and development.

LIVE HEALTHY / IMPROVE YOUR LIFESTYLE

The knowledge is the aptitude to discover an alternative.
(Bernard Jensen)

Index

DEDICATION

I am grateful to my God for giving me the opportunity
to share my knowledge with other people and for all
he has done with me.

I dedicate this book to my mother Naomi, my father Reverend
Ramon Collado, they will be always my inspiration along with
My children, Erielis, Elias, Erick, Jonathan, and my wife
Mercedes
Collado with whom I share my life and love.
My pastor Hector Fernandez Mata.
My friends of Passaic Pediatrics 2 for stimulating me
to make this book.

As well as to all those who want to have a good health.